P9-CRK-852

LE CORDON BLEU

HOME COLLECTION

·ITALIAN·

PERIPLUS
EDITIONS

contents

recipe ratings ✿ *easy* ✿✿ *a little more care needed* ✿✿✿ *more care needed*

Minestrone

Although there are many variations of this hearty soup, according to the region it comes from and the season, it will always consist of vegetables and stock with the addition of pasta or rice.

*Preparation time **45 minutes + overnight soaking***
*Total cooking time **2 hours 20 minutes***
Serves 6–8

1¼ cups dried beans, such as kidney beans or navy beans
5 oz. salt pork or slab bacon, diced
3 tablespoons olive oil
I large onion, chopped
2 carrots, diced
2 potatoes, diced
I stalk celery, diced
2 cloves garlic, chopped
I tablespoon tomato paste
3 quarts beef stock or water
bouquet garni
3 cups thinly sliced cabbage
I cup macaroni or any small pasta
grated Parmesan, to serve

1   Cover the beans with water and soak for 8 hours or overnight. Drain, put in a large saucepan with 2 quarts water and simmer for 1½ hours, or until tender.

2   Meanwhile, place the salt pork or bacon in another saucepan and cover with cold water. Bring to a boil, strain and refresh in cold water. Spread on paper towels to dry. In a large heavy-bottomed stockpot or Dutch oven, heat the olive oil and lightly brown the salt pork or bacon over medium heat for 3 minutes. Add the onion, carrots, potatoes, celery and garlic, reduce the heat and cook for 5 minutes without coloring. Add the tomato paste and cook for 3 minutes. Add the stock and simmer for 10 minutes, skimming any fat from the surface. Add the bouquet garni and cabbage and simmer for 5 minutes. Remove from the heat and set aside.

3   Drain the beans and add to the soup mixture. Return to the heat and simmer for 10 minutes. Add the pasta and cook for another 15 minutes, or until soft. Check the seasoning and remove the bouquet garni. Serve with the grated Parmesan sprinkled over the top.

Artichoke, spinach and pine nut salad

*This fresh-tasting salad could either be served as a first course,
or with crusty bread as a light lunch on a hot summer's day.*

*Preparation time **40 minutes***
*Total cooking time **30 minutes***
Serves 4

4 large fresh artichokes
juice of 2 lemons
3 cups firmly packed baby spinach leaves
1/2 cup pine nuts (pignoli), toasted
3 tablespoons olive oil
1/3 cup grated Parmesan
16 black olives, halved and pitted

1 Prepare the fresh artichokes, following the method in the Chef's techniques on page 63. When you place the artichokes in the pan of boiling water, use the juice from one of the lemons in the water. Once you have cooked and prepared the artichokes, cut them into bite-size wedges, cover and set aside.

2 In a large bowl, toss the spinach leaves with the pine nuts. Whisk the olive oil with 1 tablespoon lemon juice and freshly ground black pepper to taste, and use to dress the spinach. Divide the artichoke pieces among four bowls and pile the spinach up in the center. Top the salad with the Parmesan and black olives.

Garlic and zucchini soup

Two whole bulbs of garlic may seem a powerfully large amount, but you will find it takes on a mellow creaminess when cooked.

Preparation time **35 minutes**
Total cooking time **1 hour 15 minutes**
Serves **4–6**

olive oil, for cooking
1 onion, finely chopped
2 bulbs garlic, peeled and thinly sliced
2 potatoes, peeled and thinly sliced
2 quarts chicken stock or water
2 zucchini
1 tablespoon finely chopped fresh basil

1 Heat about 4 tablespoons of olive oil in a large heavy-bottomed saucepan, add the onion and garlic and cook over medium heat for 5–10 minutes, or until golden brown. Add the potatoes and cook for 2 minutes, stirring constantly. Add the stock, season to taste with salt and pepper and then simmer for 30 minutes. Allow to cool a little.
2 Trim the ends from the zucchini. Cut into quarters lengthwise, then cut into short pieces. Set aside.
3 Purée the soup in a blender or food processor until smooth. Return to the pan and bring to a boil. Skim any foam from the top if necessary, then add the zucchini and cook for 20–25 minutes, or until the zucchini is tender. Just before serving, stir in the basil and adjust the seasoning. Serve garnished with a few extra basil leaves.

Fritto misto with a garlic dip

*There are a number of ways to prepare Italy's well-known mixed fry. Here the fish is simply
dipped in flour, egg and then bread crumbs before being fried to a crispy golden brown.*

Preparation time ***1 hour***
Total cooking time ***20 minutes***
Serves 6 as a starter or 2 as a main course

2 shallots, finely chopped
2/3 cup dry white wine
1 bay leaf
1 sprig of fresh thyme
10 oz. fresh mussels, scrubbed and beards removed
5 oz. fresh squid (calamari)
oil, for deep-frying
4 eggs, lightly beaten
3/4 cup all-purpose flour, seasoned with salt
  and pepper
2 1/2 cups fresh bread crumbs
5 oz. plaice, sole or flounder fillet, cut into strips
5 oz. cod, ling cod or haddock fillet, cut into large,
  bite-size cubes
3/4 cup mayonnaise
1 tablespoon plain yogurt
2 cloves garlic, finely chopped
fresh parsley and lemon wedges, to garnish

1 Put the shallots, wine, bay leaf and thyme in a large
saucepan, cover and bring to a boil. Add the mussels,
discarding any that are already open, cover and reduce
to medium heat. Cook for 2 minutes, shaking the pan
occasionally, until the mussels open (discard any that do
not open). Drain and remove from the shells.
2 To prepare the fresh squid, remove the wings from
the tube, peel off the skin and remove the head. Remove
the clear cartilage quill from the opening of the tube,
cut off the tentacles and rinse the tube under running
water. Drain, dry, then slice into rings.
3 Fill a large heavy-bottomed saucepan one-third full
with oil and heat to 375°F. Put the eggs, flour and bread
crumbs into separate dishes. Toss the fish, mussels and
squid in the flour, shake off the excess, then dip into the
egg and finally coat with the bread crumbs, shaking off
the excess. Deep-fry the breaded seafood in batches
until golden brown, drain on crumpled paper towels and
sprinkle lightly with salt. If keeping warm for a few
minutes, do so on a wire rack in a warm oven, uncovered.
4 To make the garlic dip, stir together the mayonnaise,
yogurt and garlic and serve in a bowl to accompany the
seafood. Garnish with the parsley and lemon wedges.

Crostini with tapenade

Crostini are Italian canapés, ideal with soups or as an accompaniment to vegetable dishes and salads. Here they are served with a tapenade, which is very intense in flavor and should be spread thinly.

Preparation time **15 minutes**
Total cooking time **25 minutes**
Makes about 60

☼

I French baguette
olive oil, for cooking
1/2 cup pitted black olives
I small clove garlic
8 anchovy fillets

1 Preheat the oven to 350°F. Cut the bread into very thin slices. Pour enough of the oil into a large skillet to lightly coat the base and heat gently. Lightly fry the bread, in batches, on both sides, then transfer to a baking sheet. Bake in the oven until both sides are golden. Remove and cool to room temperature.
2 To make the tapenade, place the olives, garlic and anchovy fillets in a food processor and pureé to a thick paste with a spreadable consistency, adding a little olive oil if it is too dry. Season with freshly ground black pepper, but avoid salt—the saltiness of the anchovies will be enough. Spread sparingly over the crostini.

Prosciutto, smoked ham and mustard roulade

Simple to prepare, yet full of flavor, these are ideal for serving with cocktails or wine.

Preparation time **15 minutes + 10 minutes chilling**
Total cooking time **5 minutes**
Makes about 35

☼

4 oz. smoked ham pieces
1/2 cup mayonnaise
I tablespoon Dijon mustard
4 oz. prosciutto slices
3 stale petits pains (small French rolls)
fresh chervil, to garnish

1 To make the filling, purée the ham pieces in a food processor, add the mayonnaise and mustard and process to bind. Season with salt and pepper.
2 Lay the slices of prosciutto, slightly overlapping, on a sheet of plastic wrap and spread the filling mixture over the prosciutto with the back of a spoon. Roll up the prosciutto lengthwise like a jelly roll and put in the freezer for 10 minutes to firm.
3 Thinly slice the petits pains and toast until golden brown. Cut the prosciutto roll into thin slices and place a slice on each piece of toasted bread. Garnish with the fresh chervil.

Crostini with tapenade (top)
and Prosciutto, smoked ham and mustard roulade

Roman gnocchi

The extremely popular Italian gnocchi can be made from potatoes, pumpkin or, as in this case, semolina. Often served as a starter, gnocchi are also perfect for lunch, accompanied by a crisp green salad.

Preparation time **35 minutes + 30 minutes cooling**
Total cooking time **2 hours 20 minutes**
Serves 4 as a starter

3 tablespoons unsalted butter
2 oz. bacon, diced
I small onion, chopped
I small carrot, chopped
3 tablespoons tomato paste
I tablespoon all-purpose flour
I lb. tomatoes, peeled, seeded and chopped
bouquet garni
4 cloves garlic, chopped
2 cups chicken stock or water

GNOCCHI
2 cups milk
1/4 cup unsalted butter
1 1/4 cups semolina flour or fine semolina
1/4 cup all-purpose flour
3 tablespoons heavy cream
I egg
2 egg yolks
1/3 cup freshly grated Parmesan
1/3 cup unsalted butter, melted

1 Preheat the oven to 350°F. Melt the butter in a small flameproof casserole and cook the bacon until golden brown. Add the onion and carrot and cook for 3 minutes. Stir in the tomato paste and cook for 2 minutes. Sprinkle with the flour, place in the oven for 5 minutes, then stir until the flour disappears. Add the tomatoes, bouquet garni and garlic, return to the stove top and cook for 5 minutes, stirring. Stir in the stock and boil for 2 minutes. Cover and bake in the oven for 1 hour. Strain into a clean saucepan and discard the solids. Bring the sauce back to a boil on the stove top and skim if necessary. Lower the heat and simmer for 20 minutes, or until thickened. Season to taste with salt and black pepper, set aside and keep warm.

2 To make the gnocchi, bring the milk and butter to a boil in a large saucepan. Add the flours and stir over low heat until absorbed, then stir for 5 minutes longer, or until the mixture rolls off the side of the pan. Remove from the heat, add the cream, egg, egg yolks and half the Parmesan and stir until smooth. Season to taste, and spread 1/2-inch thick on a baking sheet lined with waxed paper. Cool for 30 minutes, then cut into rounds with a wet 1 1/2-inch cutter. Put in a baking dish, drizzle with the melted butter and sprinkle with the remaining Parmesan. Bake for 20 minutes, or until golden, and serve with the tomato sauce.

Parmesan tulips with eggplant caviar

Although rather time-consuming to prepare, the beautiful presentation of this dish, combining colors and complementary flavors, will make an impressive start to any meal.

Preparation time **25 minutes + 30 minutes marinating + 1 hour refrigeration**
Total cooking time **1 hour**
Makes 10

4 red bell peppers
I teaspoon lemon juice
¹/3 cup olive oil
I ¹/2 cups grated Parmesan

EGGPLANT CAVIAR
1³/4 lb. eggplant
¹/4 cup olive oil
¹/3 cup pitted and chopped black olives
I clove garlic, crushed
2–3 tablespoons finely chopped fresh chives
¹/2 teaspoon paprika

1 Halve the peppers, removing the seeds and membrane. Place in a dish and sprinkle with salt and freshly ground black pepper. Stir the lemon juice into the olive oil, pour over the peppers, cover and marinate for at least 30 minutes and up to 2 hours. Preheat the oven to 350°F.

2 To make the eggplant caviar, cut the eggplants in half lengthwise. Brush the cut side with a little of the olive oil and sprinkle with salt and pepper. Place on a baking sheet and bake for 25 minutes, or until soft. Drain to remove the liquid and scrape out the flesh with a spoon. Coarsely chop the flesh and combine with the olives, garlic and chives, reserving some chives for the garnish. Mix well with a fork, squeezing the eggplant against the side of the bowl to break it down. Add the remaining olive oil very slowly, stirring it in with the fork. Add the paprika and season to taste. Refrigerate for 1 hour.

3 To make the Parmesan tulips, draw two 4-inch circles on a piece of waxed paper and place on a baking sheet. Sprinkle a thick layer of Parmesan in each circle. Bake for 3–5 minutes, or until bubbled with light golden-brown edges. Cool for a few moments, then lift off with a flexible metal spatula. Shape into tulips by molding over the top of a bottle neck, pleating the edges and holding in place until cooled. Repeat with the remaining Parmesan.

4 Preheat a barbecue grill or broiler, brush with oil and cook the peppers for 5 minutes each side, or until tender. Remove the skin and cut the peppers into strips. Place a heaped tablespoon of eggplant caviar in each Parmesan tulip and sprinkle with the reserved chives. Arrange the peppers in crosses around the tulips and serve immediately.

Bruschetta with prosciutto, Gorgonzola and sun-dried tomatoes

Italians are great bread-eaters. Bruschetta are thin slices of bread, broiled and rubbed with a clove of cut garlic—the original garlic bread.

Preparation time **10 minutes**
Total cooking time **5 minutes**
Makes **8**

1 loaf Italian bread
2 cloves garlic, halved
1/4 cup extra virgin olive oil
8 sun-dried tomatoes in olive oil
6 oz. Gorgonzola cheese
4 slices prosciutto, cut in half

1 To prepare the bruschetta, cut the bread into thin slices and broil or toast to golden brown. Rub one side of each slice with the cut surface of the garlic. Drizzle with the olive oil and sprinkle with salt and freshly ground black pepper.

2 Drain the sun-dried tomatoes, scrape off any seeds and cut into thin strips. Press or spread the cheese onto the bruschetta, lay the prosciutto on top and garnish with strips of tomato. Season with a few gridings of freshly ground black pepper and serve.

Chef's tips If Gorgonzola is too strong for your taste, use the creamier, milder Dolcelatte instead.

As a variation, marinate diced fresh tomatoes, garlic, and chopped fresh basil leaves in enough balsamic vinegar to moisten well. Drain the excess juice and place a spoonful on top of the warm slice of bruschetta.

Tomato and balsamic vinegar salad

*The syrupy balsamic vinegar used in this salad is made in the Modena area
and gives a delicious, rich bittersweet flavor to the dressing.*

Preparation time **15 minutes**
Total cooking time **None**
Serves 6–8

1 clove garlic, finely chopped
¹/4 cup balsamic vinegar
¹/2 cup extra virgin olive oil
6 ripe tomatoes
2 small shallots, finely chopped
2–3 tablespoons fresh basil leaves, finely chopped
fresh basil leaves, to garnish

1 Place the garlic in a small bowl. Add a good pinch of salt and freshly ground black pepper. Whisk in the balsamic vinegar, then gradually whisk in the olive oil until the sauce is thick and completely combined.

2 Remove the stem ends from the tomatoes and cut the tomatoes either into thin wedges or slices. Sprinkle the bottom of a serving plate with salt and freshly ground black pepper and arrange the cut tomatoes over this. Sprinkle with the shallots and chopped basil leaves. Drizzle the vinaigrette over the tomatoes and decorate with the whole basil leaves. Keep in the refrigerator until ready to serve.

Chef's tip If you are preparing this salad ahead of time, keep in mind that the tomatoes, in contact with the salt, will begin to release their juices. If this should happen, tilt the serving plate to let the liquid run off. Wipe the edges of the plate and drizzle a little more vinaigrette over the tomatoes before serving.

Broiled scallops with prosciutto

A simple dish combining fresh, flavorful ingredients guaranteed to delight and impress your guests.
Be careful not to overcook the prosciutto, which would cause it to become too salty.

*Preparation time **20 minutes + 20 minutes cooling***
*Total cooking time **10 minutes***
Serves 4 as a starter

¼ cup sugar
finely grated rind of ½ lemon
sprig of fresh rosemary
12 slices prosciutto
12 large fresh or frozen thawed scallops, patted dry
 (see Chef's tips)
⅓ cup pitted and chopped black olives
2 plum tomatoes, peeled, seeded and diced
2 tablespoons drained capers
I clove garlic, chopped
2 tablespoons chopped fresh chives
olive oil

1 Put the sugar in a small saucepan with ⅓ cup water and heat gently, stirring to dissolve. Add the lemon rind and rosemary, increase the heat and boil for 2 minutes. Remove from the heat and leave to cool for about 20 minutes.

2 Lay the prosciutto slices on a work surface. Brush the scallops with the lemon and rosemary syrup and place one on each piece of prosciutto. Wrap the prosciutto around the scallop and secure with string or a skewer.

3 Make a relish by mixing together the olives, diced tomatoes, capers, garlic and 1 tablespoon of the chives. Pour in enough olive oil to bind the mixture together.

4 Brush the wrapped scallops with the olive oil and either quickly brown under a preheated hot broiler or fry in a nonstick skillet for 1–2 minutes each side. Remove the string or skewer, then serve the scallops with a little relish beside them.

Chef's tips If using fresh scallops in their shells, remove them by sliding a knife under the white muscle and orange roe. Wash the scallops to remove any grit or sand, then pull away and discard the small, tough, shiny white muscle and the black vein, leaving the orange roe intact. Dry the scallops on paper towels.

This recipe is also wonderful with monkfish. You will need a 2 lb. piece of fish (ask your fish merchant to skin and fillet it). Use the same method as for the scallops, brushing the fish with syrup and wrapping the whole fish in prosciutto. Quickly brown under the broiler or in a nonstick skillet, then bake in a 400°F oven for 5–8 minutes. Cover loosely with aluminum foil and leave to rest for 5 minutes before slicing and serving.

Mushroom ravioli in rosemary garlic cream

Ideal as a first course or for a light lunch, the creamy sauce in this dish
truly complements the ravioli with its tasty mushroom filling.

Preparation time *1 hour + 20 minutes cooling*
Total cooking time *45 minutes*
Serves *4 as a starter*

PASTA
1 cup all-purpose flour
pinch of salt
1 teaspoon oil
1 egg, lightly beaten

MUSHROOM FILLING
olive oil, for cooking
2 shallots, finely chopped
5 oz. button or wild mushrooms (about 15 button),
   chopped
3 tablespoons fresh bread crumbs
1/4 cup each of chopped fresh chervil, thyme, flat-leaf
   parsley and basil

2 cups chicken stock
8 cloves garlic, coarsely chopped
large sprig of fresh rosemary, cut into pieces
2 cups heavy cream
beaten egg, to glaze
Parmesan shavings, to garnish

1 To make the pasta, follow the method in the Chef's techniques on page 62, dividing the dough into two pieces before passing through the pasta machine.
2 To make the filling, heat a little oil over low heat and cook the shallots for 3 minutes. Add the mushrooms and a good pinch of salt. Cook, stirring, for 10 minutes, or until the mushrooms are dry. Season to taste, then mix in the bread crumbs, herbs and enough olive oil to just bind the mixture. Set aside.
3 To make the sauce, cook the stock and garlic over high heat for 20 minutes, or until syrupy. Remove from the heat, add the rosemary and leave to cool for about 20 minutes. Remove the rosemary, transfer the sauce to a blender or food processor and blend until smooth. Strain into a small saucepan, add the cream and simmer for 5 minutes, or until thick enough to coat the back of a spoon. Season and keep warm.
4 Mark one strip of the pasta dough with a round 1 1/2-inch biscuit cutter. Place a little filling in the center of each mark. Lightly brush around the filling with beaten egg. Place the second sheet of dough over the first sheet. Squeeze any air from between the ravioli and use the pastry cutter to cut and seal the dough.
5 Bring a large saucepan of salted water to a boil. Cook the ravioli for 2–3 minutes, or until *al dente*. Strain and serve with the sauce and shavings of Parmesan.

Seafood risotto

*Despite being a rather time-consuming dish to make, the final combination
of fresh seafood with creamy risotto rice is well worth the effort.*

Preparation time **55 minutes**
Total cooking time **1 hour 20 minutes**
Serves 8

1 lb. fresh mussels
8 oz. fresh or frozen thawed scallops, patted dry
(see Chef's tip)
1 lb. raw shrimp, shells on
3 cups white wine
1 onion, coarsely chopped
1 bay leaf
2 sprigs of fresh thyme
olive oil, for cooking
4 shallots, roughly chopped
1 stalk celery, coarsely chopped
1 small carrot, coarsely chopped
8 cloves garlic, coarsely chopped
1 onion, finely chopped
2 cups arborio rice
1/2 cup heavy cream
2/3 cup grated Parmesan
2 tablespoons chopped fresh parsley
Parmesan shavings and lemon wedges, to garnish

1 Scrub the mussels, remove the beards and discard
any open mussels. Dry the scallops and set aside. Peel
and devein the shrimp, keeping the shells and any heads.
2 Put the mussels, 2 cups of the wine, the coarsely
chopped onion, bay leaf and thyme in a large saucepan,
cover and bring to a boil. Cook for 5 minutes, or until
the mussels have opened. Remove the mussels and set
aside to cool, discarding any that haven't opened. Strain
the cooking liquid through a fine sieve lined with a
clean piece of cheesecloth.
3 Heat about 1/4 cup olive oil in a large pan and cook
the shelled shrimp over high heat for 2 minutes, or until
pink. Remove with a slotted spoon and set aside. Add
the scallops and cook for 2 minutes, then drain and set
aside. Add the shrimp heads and shells and cook for
2–3 minutes, or until pink, crushing with a large spoon
or potato masher. Add the shallots, celery, carrot and
half the garlic and cook for 2 minutes. Add the cooking
liquid from the mussels and boil for 15 minutes. Add
2 cups water, bring to a boil and cook for 10 minutes.
Strain the liquid, pressing the solids to extract as much
flavor as possible. Add enough water to the liquid to
make up 7 cups and return to the pan. Bring to a boil,
then reduce the heat and maintain the stock at a very
low simmer.
4 Heat about 1/4 cup of the oil over medium-low heat
in a large heavy-bottomed saucepan and cook the finely
chopped onion for 3–5 minutes, or until soft and
translucent. Add the rice and remaining garlic and stir
well with a wooden spoon, making sure that the rice
is completely coated with oil. Cook for 2 minutes, then
add the rest of the wine, stirring well. Cook over
low heat, stirring constantly, until the wine has been
absorbed. Add 1 cup of the hot stock, stirring frequently
until the liquid has been almost completely absorbed
before adding another 1 cup of stock. Continue for
30–35 minutes, or until all the stock has been added and
the rice is tender, stirring constantly to keep the rice
from sticking to the bottom. Mix in the cream and
Parmesan, adjust the seasoning and remove from the
heat. Stir in the shrimp, scallops, mussels and the
chopped parsley and serve with the Parmesan shavings
and some lemon wedges on the side.

Chef's tip If using fresh scallops, wash to remove any
grit or sand, then pull away the small, tough, shiny white
muscle and the black vein, leaving the orange roe intact.

Tagliatelle with mushrooms and leeks

While freshly made pasta will give the best results in this recipe, dried pasta could be substituted if time is short. If buying dried pasta, try to choose a good-quality pasta made from durum wheat flour only.

Preparation time **45 minutes**
Total cooking time **15 minutes**
Serves 4

PASTA
2¹/2 cups all-purpose flour
I teaspoon salt
2 tablespoons olive oil
3 eggs, lightly beaten

¹/4 cup unsalted butter
2 cups assorted fresh mushrooms, such as cèpes,
 chanterelles, cremini, sliced
3 shallots, chopped
juice of ¹/2 lemon
¹/4 cup fresh parsley, chopped
2 tablespoons sherry
8 baby leeks or 2 medium leeks, sliced
³/4 cup unsalted butter, chilled and cut
 into cubes

1 To make the pasta, follow the method in the Chef's techniques on page 62, dividing the dough into four pieces before passing through the pasta machine. When the pasta has passed through the thinnest setting on the machine, pass the sheets of dough through the ¹/4-inch cutters to make tagliatelle.

2 Heat the butter in a skillet, add the mushrooms and cook until starting to color. Toss in the shallots and cook for 2–3 minutes. Add the lemon juice, parsley and sherry. Season, set aside and keep warm. Cook the leeks in boiling salted water for 2 minutes, then drain.

3 Half fill a small saucepan with water, bring to a boil, then remove from the heat. Place a heatproof bowl over the pan and pour in ¹/3 cup boiling water. Whisk in the cubes of butter, piece by piece. Remove the bowl and whisk the sauce for 1 minute. Season to taste with salt and pepper, add the leeks, cover and keep warm.

4 Cook the pasta in boiling salted water for 2 minutes, or until *al dente*. Drain, pile high on individual plates, top with the mushrooms and spoon the leek and butter sauce around.

Chef's tip If cutting the pasta by hand, after kneading and refrigerating, divide the dough into four pieces, roll each into a rectangle or circle as thinly as possible and cut into strips using a sharp knife. Lay in a single layer on a lightly floured dish towel hanging over the back of a chair until ready to use.

Veal parmigiana

This dish from northern Italy successfully combines the delicacy of veal with the strong, tangy flavor of Parmesan.

*Preparation time **45 minutes***
*Total cooking time **1 hour 40 minutes***
Serves 4

2 lb. large ripe tomatoes
2–3 small sprigs of fresh basil
1 bay leaf
2 sprigs of fresh thyme
olive oil, for cooking
1 onion, finely chopped
3 cloves garlic, finely chopped
4 veal scallops, about 4 oz. each
all-purpose flour, seasoned with salt and pepper,
**   to coat**
2 eggs, lightly beaten
1²/3 cups fresh bread crumbs
1/3 cup grated Parmesan
1 tablespoon finely chopped fresh parsley
1/2 cup unsalted butter
8 oz. mozzarella cheese, sliced

1 Score a cross in the base of each tomato. Place in a bowl of boiling water for 10 seconds, then plunge into cold water and peel the skin away from the cross. Cut the tomatoes in half horizontally and remove the seeds with the handle of a small spoon. Chop coarsely. Pull the basil leaves from their stems. Tie the stems with the bay leaf and thyme to make a bouquet garni.

2 Heat 1/4 cup olive oil in a saucepan and slowly cook the onion for 5 minutes without coloring. Add the tomatoes, garlic and bouquet garni. Season and simmer, covered, for 20 minutes, then uncovered for 45 minutes. Remove the bouquet garni and adjust the seasoning to taste.

3 Pound the veal with a meat mallet until 1/8 inch thick. Coat in the flour, shaking off the excess. Dip the coated veal in the beaten egg.

4 Mix together the bread crumbs, Parmesan and parsley in a shallow dish. Drain any excess egg from the veal and then coat with the bread crumb mixture, pressing well with your fingers to make it stick.

5 Preheat the oven to 400°F. Heat about 1/2 cup oil in a large nonstick skillet. Add half the butter and, when it is foaming, cook two pieces of veal for about 3 minutes, or until golden brown, turning once. Drain on paper towels. Discard any leftover oil and butter from the pan and cook the remaining veal in fresh oil and butter. Arrange the veal in a baking dish, cover with the mozzarella and bake for 10 minutes, or until the cheese has melted. Serve with the tomato sauce on top, garnished with the fresh basil leaves.

Cannelloni with spinach

These pasta tubes may be stuffed with a variety of fillings, whether meat, cheese or vegetable. In this recipe they are filled with spinach, coated with a creamy white sauce and baked in the oven until golden brown.

Preparation time 1 hour + 20 minutes refrigeration
Total cooking time 55 minutes
Serves 8–10 (see Chef's tips)

❁ ❁

PASTA
1²/₃ cups all-purpose flour
¹/₂ teaspoon salt
4 teaspoons olive oil
2 eggs, lightly beaten

1 small onion, studded with a whole clove
1 quart milk
1 bay leaf
¹/₃ cup unsalted butter
¹/₃ cup all-purpose flour
1 teaspoon powdered mustard
1 clove garlic, finely chopped
2 lb. fresh spinach, coarsely chopped
pinch of grated nutmeg
2 egg yolks
¹/₃ cup grated Parmesan
¹/₃ cup fresh bread crumbs

1 To make the pasta, follow the method in the Chef's techniques on page 62, dividing the dough into two pieces before passing through the pasta machine. Roll the dough out thinly on a lightly floured surface and cut into sixteen 4 x 3-inch pieces. Soften in boiling salted water, a few at a time, for 1 minute. Remove with a slotted spoon and refresh in cold water to stop the cooking. Lay the sheets on a clean towel to drain.

2 Put the onion in a saucepan with the milk and bay leaf. Bring slowly almost to a boil, then remove from the heat, strain and set aside. Melt 3 tablespoons of the butter in a saucepan, remove from the heat and stir in the flour. Cook over low heat for 1–2 minutes, remove from the heat, stir in the mustard and season. Whisk in the hot milk gradually until smooth. Return to the heat and simmer, stirring, for 10 minutes, or until thick enough to coat the back of a spoon. Remove from the heat. Press buttered waxed paper onto the surface to prevent a skin from forming, cover and set aside. Preheat the oven to 375°F.

3 Melt the remaining butter over low heat and cook the garlic until softened but not colored. Add the spinach, cover and cook over medium heat until just wilted. Season with salt, pepper and the nutmeg. Drain, return to the pan and stir in the yolks, half the Parmesan and enough of the white sauce to bind it together.

4 Lay the pasta on a board. Spoon the filling along the center of each piece and roll up. Place in a buttered baking dish and coat with the rest of the sauce. Sprinkle with the remaining Parmesan mixed with the bread crumbs. Bake for 20–25 minutes, or until golden.

Chef's tips It is difficult to make a smaller quantity of pasta. This recipe serves 8–10 people, so if you find this is too much, make it in two smaller dishes and freeze one for another time.

Instead of the fresh pasta, you could use 15–20 dried cannelloni tubes.

Osso buco

A specialty of Milan, this dish is best made using shank from the hind leg. The pieces should be cut no thicker than suggested, to guarantee tenderness. Savor the bone marrow, supposedly the best part of this dish.

*Preparation time **45 minutes***
*Total cooking time **2 hours 30 minutes***
Serves 4

4 veal shank cross cuts, about 1 1/2 inches thick (osso buco)
all-purpose flour, seasoned with salt and pepper
oil, for cooking
3 tablespoons unsalted butter
1 carrot, sliced
1 stalk celery, sliced
1 onion, sliced
4 cloves garlic, chopped
8 tomatoes, peeled, seeded and chopped
1 cup white wine
bouquet garni
1 quart beef stock or water
2 tablespoons chopped fresh parsley
rind of 1/4 orange, finely chopped
rind of 1/4 lemon, finely chopped

1 Preheat the oven to 350°F. Trim the meat of any sinew or skin and lightly coat with the seasoned flour.

Heat a little oil in a small nonstick skillet and brown the veal on both sides, in batches if necessary. Set aside.

2 Melt the butter in a flameproof casserole or Dutch oven and cook the carrot, celery and onion over medium heat for 3 minutes. Add the garlic and mix well, then add the chopped tomatoes and cook for 5 minutes. Add the white wine and bouquet garni and cook for another 5 minutes. Add the stock and the browned meat, bring to a simmer, season, cover and bake for 1 1/2 hours, or until the meat is tender.

3 Transfer the meat to a serving platter, cover and keep warm. Heat the cooking liquid and vegetables and bring to a boil. Skim off any fat or foam that rises to the top and cook for 20–25 minutes, or until the sauce has thickened and coats the back of a spoon. Stir in the parsley, orange and lemon rind and season to taste. Simmer for another 5 minutes, then pour over the meat and serve immediately.

Chef's tip If you prefer a milder citrus flavor, blanch the orange and lemon rinds before using. Place the rinds in a small saucepan and cover with cold water, bring to a boil for 30 seconds, then strain and refresh. Use as instructed in the recipe.

Pasta with prosciutto and Parmesan

This simple pasta dish makes the most of two of Italy's most famous ingredients—prosciutto, a salt-cured ham, and the rich, grainy Parmesan. As both of these ingredients are salty, particular care should be taken when seasoning this dish.

Preparation time **20 minutes**
Total cooking time **20 minutes**
Serves 4

¼ cup olive oil
12 oz. farfalle (pasta bows)
1 large onion, thinly sliced
18 button mushrooms, thinly sliced
3 zucchini, cut into short sticks
1 large clove garlic, chopped
5 oz. prosciutto, cut into strips
1¼ cups crème fraîche
1 cup grated Parmesan
fresh basil leaves, to garnish

1 Bring a large saucepan two-thirds full of water to a boil. Add a good pinch of salt and 1 tablespoon of the olive oil. Add the farfalle to the bubbling water, stir with a fork and cook according to the manufacturer's instructions until the pasta is *al dente*. Pour immediately into a colander, then refresh under plenty of cold running water. Leave to drain until needed.

2 Heat a saucepan over high heat and add the rest of the olive oil. When the oil is hot, add the onion, mushrooms, zucchini and garlic and fry for about 2 minutes, or until the vegetables are lightly colored. Reduce the heat, add the prosciutto strips and fry for 2–3 minutes. Stir in the crème fraîche and heat the mixture for another 2 minutes. Stir in the grated Parmesan and season to taste with salt and freshly ground black pepper.

3 Add the pasta to the pan, stir to combine and cook briefly to make sure the pasta is heated through. Serve immediately with the fresh basil leaves sprinkled over the pasta.

Veal with lemon and capers

The capers and lemon provide a sharp contrast to the buttery sauce in this classic Italian dish.

*Preparation time **20 minutes***
*Total cooking time **25 minutes***
Serves 4

4 veal scallops, about 4 oz. each
all-purpose flour, seasoned with salt and pepper
2 eggs, beaten
3 tablespoons oil
3 tablespoons unsalted butter
I cup white wine
1/4 cup capers, rinsed and drained
I cup chicken or veal stock
I–2 tablespoons lemon juice
1/2 cup unsalted butter, chilled and cubed

1 Pound the meat with a mallet until it is 1/8 inch thick, then cut into thirds and coat with the seasoned flour. Put the beaten egg in a bowl and mix together with 2 tablespoons water. Coat the veal in the egg mixture, draining off any excess.

2 Heat the oil and butter in a nonstick skillet. Cook the veal, in batches, for 3–5 minutes, until golden brown on both sides. Drain on paper towels, cover and keep warm while cooking the other veal slices.

3 Pour off the oil from the pan, add the wine and capers and cook for 8 minutes, or until almost dry. Add the stock and cook for 5 minutes, or until reduced by half. Add 1 tablespoon lemon juice, then transfer the sauce to a small saucepan (keeping the skillet on one side). Whisk in the cubes of butter, without allowing the sauce to boil. Adjust the seasoning, adding more lemon juice if necessary. Transfer the veal to the skillet, pour in the sauce, cover and leave for 2 minutes before serving.

Venetian-style liver

Tender calf's liver, rich in iron, protein and vitamin A, has a mild flavor that is perfectly enhanced by the soft caramelized onions in this Venetian recipe.

Preparation time **20 minutes**
Total cooking time **30 minutes**
Serves 4

1 lb. calf's liver, sliced
vegetable oil, for cooking
2 medium onions, thinly sliced

1 Make sure the liver is completely free of veins and remove any of the thin skin that may still be attached.
2 Heat 2–3 tablespoons of oil in a large nonstick skillet and add the onion and a large pinch of salt. Cook over medium heat for 20–30 minutes, or until the onions are completely soft and golden brown. Remove the onions with a slotted spoon, leaving the oil in the skillet.
3 Add a little more oil to the skillet if necessary and heat until lightly smoking. Fry the liver in small batches, just enough to cover the base of the pan, for 1 minute, or until it has changed color from pink to brown. Toss and cook for a moment more. Transfer each batch to a warm plate and season to taste with salt and freshly ground black pepper.
4 Return all the liver to the pan, add the cooked onions and toss to combine, but not to cook further. Transfer to a warm serving plate and serve immediately with steamed spinach and a simple risotto alongside.

Chef's tip The liver must fry very quickly to retain its succulence, therefore it is very important that the pan is hot or the liver will stick and fry for too long. Don't try to rush by cooking the liver in large batches—too much meat will overcrowd the pan, making the temperature drop and the liver stew rather than fry.

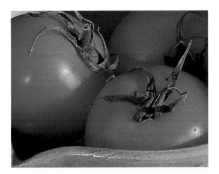

Rabbit and marjoram stew with herb biscuits

Italians are very fond of game, and rabbit, with its light and tender flesh, is definitely a favorite. Here it is teamed with fresh herbs, both in the stew and in the biscuits placed on top to soak up the flavorful juices.

Preparation time **40 minutes**
Total cooking time **1 hour 30 minutes**
Serves 4

1 rabbit, weighing 2¹/₂ lb., cut into 8 pieces
all-purpose flour, seasoned with salt and pepper
butter or oil, for cooking
1 onion, finely chopped
1²/₃ cups sliced button mushrooms
1 teaspoon tomato paste
1 clove garlic, chopped
2 cups chicken stock
8 ripe tomatoes, peeled, seeded and chopped
1 tablespoon chopped fresh rosemary
2 tablespoons chopped fresh marjoram
1 tablespoon chopped fresh parsley

HERB BISCUITS
2 cups self-rising flour
2 teaspoons sugar
¹/₃ cup unsalted butter, chilled and cut into cubes
1 tablespoon chopped fresh herbs, such as parsley,
   rosemary, thyme or marjoram
¹/₂ cup buttermilk
1 egg, beaten

1 Coat the rabbit in the flour. Heat a little butter or oil in a skillet, brown the rabbit on all sides, then remove from the pan and drain on paper towels. Add the onion to the pan and cook over low heat until soft. Add the mushrooms, increase the heat and stir in the tomato paste and garlic. Transfer to a flameproof casserole or Dutch oven, add the rabbit and season with salt and black pepper.

2 Pour in the stock (it should be enough to barely cover the rabbit) and simmer gently on the stove top for 30 minutes. Add the tomatoes and cook for another 10 minutes. Add the rosemary, marjoram and parsley. Check that the meat is tender and season to taste.

3 To make the biscuits, preheat the oven to 400°F. Sift the flour, sugar and a good pinch of salt into a large bowl, add the butter and cut it in until crumbly. Toss in the herbs, then stir in the milk until the dry flour has disappeared and the mixture is in large lumps. Turn out onto a lightly floured surface and gather together into a smooth ball. Roll or pat out to a ⁵/₈-inch thickness. Work quickly—you want the dough to rise in the oven, not waste its rising power while it's being rolled. Cut into 1¹/₂-inch rounds, brush the tops with the egg and arrange immediately over the rabbit stew. Place the casserole on the top rack of the oven and bake for 12 minutes, or until the biscuits are golden.

Classic lasagna

*Although you can make this very popular classic Italian dish with store-bought lasagna noodles,
the flavor and texture of thinly rolled fresh pasta is quite unique and well worth the effort.*

Preparation time **1 hour + 20 minutes resting**
Total cooking time **2 hours 15 minutes**
Serves 10–12

olive oil, for cooking
2 lb. lean ground beef
1 large onion, finely chopped
8 cloves garlic, finely chopped
**4 x 16 oz. cans peeled plum tomatoes, undrained and
   puréed in a food mill or processor**
1/2 cup red wine
1/4 cup tomato paste
4 sprigs of fresh thyme
1 bay leaf
1 1/4 lb. ricotta cheese
1/3 cup heavy cream
4 eggs
12 oz. mozzarella cheese, thinly sliced
1/2 cup freshly grated Parmesan

PASTA
3 1/3 cups all-purpose flour
1 teaspoon salt
3 tablespoons olive oil
4 eggs

1 Heat 2 tablespoons oil in a large saucepan until very hot. Add the beef and brown for 10 minutes, or until the liquid has almost evaporated. Strain off the fat and set the meat aside. Reduce the heat to low, heat a little more oil and cook the onion for 5 minutes, without coloring. Add the garlic, tomatoes, wine, tomato paste, thyme, bay leaf and beef and simmer for 45 minutes to 1 hour, or until the liquid has reduced by half.

2 To make the pasta, follow the method in the Chef's techniques on page 62, dividing the dough into four pieces before passing through the pasta machine. Drain the ricotta in a sieve, then mix with the cream and eggs in a large bowl. Season, cover and set aside. Preheat the oven to 375°F.

3 Roll out the pasta dough to about 1/16 to 1/8 inch thick and cut into 5 x 4-inch rectangles. Blanch two or three noodles at a time briefly in boiling salted water, then drain on clean towels.

4 Spread about 3/4 cup of the meat sauce in a 9 x 13-inch baking dish. Arrange a layer of pasta on top and cover with a third of the cheese mixture, then another layer of meat sauce. Repeat the layers twice more and finish with a layer of pasta covered with meat sauce. Cover with mozzarella and sprinkle with Parmesan. Bake for 45 minutes, or until golden brown. Leave to rest for 20 minutes before cutting.

Chicken cacciatore

Literally meaning "hunter-style" chicken, this ever popular dish combines the flavors of mushrooms, sweet bell peppers and onions with herbs in a rich tomato sauce.

Preparation time **30 minutes**
Total cooking time **1 hour**
Serves 4

1/4 cup olive oil
I chicken, weighing about 31/4 lb.,
   cut into 8 pieces
2 medium onions, thinly sliced
   into rings
I clove garlic, finely chopped
I 1/4 cups thinly sliced button mushrooms
I small green bell pepper, thinly sliced
1/4 cup tomato paste
3/4 cup dry white wine
16 oz. canned plum tomatoes
1/2 teaspoon dried rosemary
1/2 teaspoon dried oregano

1 Heat the olive oil in a large skillet. Season the chicken with salt and pepper, then fry, skin-side-down, for 5 minutes, or until lightly browned. Turn over and brown the other side. Remove and set aside.

2 Add the onions to the pan and cook for 5 minutes, then add the garlic, mushrooms and pepper. Cook for another 3–4 minutes, or until the onions are golden. Mix in the tomato paste and cook for 1–2 minutes, then add the wine. Bring to a boil, stirring constantly, then add the tomatoes, breaking them down with a wooden spoon. Sprinkle in the rosemary and oregano and return the chicken to the pan. Season with salt and pepper, cover and simmer for 20 minutes, stirring occasionally.

3 Check the chicken to see if it is tender—if not, cover and cook for another 10 minutes—then transfer with a slotted spoon to a serving plate. If the sauce appears too liquid, allow to boil, uncovered, for 5 minutes. Season to taste, then pour over the chicken. Serve immediately.

Mediterranean vegetables with polenta cakes

Polenta features strongly in the diet of northern Italy. Traditionally cut into slices with string once cooled and set, here it is fried in melted butter and served with a delicious, soft mixture of Mediterranean vegetables.

Preparation time **35 minutes + chilling**
Total cooking time **1 hour**
Serves 6

2¹/₄ cups milk
1¹/₂ cups instant polenta
2 tablespoons unsalted butter
¹/₃ cup grated Parmesan
1 small red bell pepper, halved and seeded
1 small green bell pepper, halved and seeded
1 small yellow bell pepper, halved and seeded
olive oil and butter, for cooking
1 small zucchini, cubed
1 small eggplant, cubed
1 small red onion, cubed
³/₄ cup sun-dried tomatoes in oil, diced
4 cloves garlic, crushed
2 tablespoons canned chopped tomatoes, strained

MINT AND PISTACHIO DRESSING
¹/₄ cup milk
¹/₄ cup shelled and skinned pistachios
1¹/₂ cups fresh mint leaves
3 tablespoons pistachio or olive oil
1 clove garlic, chopped

1 Bring the milk to a boil in a deep-sided pan and whisk in the polenta. Lower the heat and cook gently, stirring occasionally, for 5 minutes, or until smooth. Stir in the butter, Parmesan and salt and pepper to taste. Turn out onto a greased baking sheet and spread out to a ⁵/₈-inch thickness. Leave to cool, then chill until set.
2 Brush the skin of the peppers with a little oil and place, skin-side-up, under a hot broiler until blackened. Put in a plastic bag for 5 minutes, then peel away the skin. Cut the flesh into cubes.
3 To make the dressing, bring the milk to a boil. Remove from the heat and transfer to a food processor with the pistachios, mint, oil and garlic. Lightly process, leaving small pieces of nut and mint in the mixture.
4 Heat a little olive oil in a large skillet, add the vegetables, sun-dried tomato and garlic and toss over the heat for 8 minutes, or until tender. Add a little dressing to moisten, and 1 tablespoon of the strained tomatoes. Season and keep warm.
5 Cut the polenta into 3-inch rounds with a pastry cutter or cup, then fry in a little melted butter until golden brown on both sides. Serve the polenta cakes topped with the vegetables and some mint and pistachio dressing. Arrange the remaining dressing and strained tomato around and garnish with a few extra mint leaves to serve.

Sicilian cheesecake

This baked ricotta cheesecake with its light cake base, citrus filling and a hint of spice is the perfect dessert to end any traditional Italian meal.

Preparation time **30 minutes + 15 minutes cooling**
Total cooking time **1 hour 35 minutes**
Serves 10

❋ ❋

SPONGE CAKE
3 eggs
1/3 cup sugar
3/4 cup all-purpose flour
1 tablespoon unsalted butter, melted, but cooled

2 1/2 cups milk
1 cup vermicelli, crushed
1/3 cup plus 1 1/2 tablespoons sugar
6 eggs, separated
12 oz. ricotta cheese
large pinch of ground cinnamon
finely grated rind of 1 lemon
1/4 cup orange-flower water
2/3 cup finely chopped mixed candied citrus peel or citron
rind of 1 lemon, cut into fine strips
1/4 cup confectioners' sugar, to garnish

1 Preheat the oven to 375°F. Grease the base and sides of a 9-inch springform pan. To make the cake, follow the method for preparing enriched sponge cake in the Chef's techniques on page 63, then pour the mixture into the pan.

2 Bake for 20 minutes, or until the center of the cake just springs back at the light touch of a finger. Turn out onto a wire rack to cool. Trim a layer from the top and bottom of the cake and discard. Return the cake to the pan.

3 Put the milk in a saucepan, bring just to a boil and add the vermicelli, a pinch of salt and the 1 1/2 tablespoons of sugar. Simmer for 25 minutes, or until the milk has been completely absorbed. Remove from the heat, leave to cool for about 15 minutes, then stir in the egg yolks. Lightly beat the ricotta in a bowl with the cinnamon, grated lemon rind, orange-flower water, candied peel and half of the remaining sugar. Add the vermicelli mixture.

4 Beat the egg whites until firm peaks form. Add the remaining sugar and beat until stiff and shiny. Fold into the ricotta mixture and pour over the cake. Sprinkle with the lemon strips and bake for 45 minutes, or until firm. Leave in the pan for 5 minutes before removing the springform ring and inverting it onto a wire rack. Loosen the base of the pan and lift off the cake. Allow to cool completely. Dust with sifted confectioners' sugar to serve.

Zuccotto

*A crisp coating of chocolate hides a liqueur-soaked sponge and a double layer of
cream and chocolate filling with cherries and nuts. Reminiscent of the wonderful ice-cream cakes
of Italy, which surprise you with the different flavors of each melting mouthful.*

Preparation time **45 minutes + chilling**
Total cooking time **30 minutes**
Serves **8**

SPONGE CAKE
3 eggs
1/2 cup sugar
3/4 cup all-purpose flour
1/4 cup cocoa powder
1 1/2 tablespoons unsalted butter, melted,
  but cooled

2 tablespoons maraschino liqueur or Kirsch
2 tablespoons brandy
1 1/4 cups heavy cream
1/3 cup confectioners' sugar
1/3 cup almonds, toasted and finely chopped
  (see Chef's tips)
1/3 cup hazelnuts, toasted and chopped
  (see Chef's tips)
1/3 cup chopped good-quality semisweet chocolate
1/4 cup chopped glacé (candied) cherries, chopped
10 oz. good-quality semisweet chocolate, melted
  (see Chef's tips)
1/4 cup chopped white chocolate

1 Preheat the oven to 350°F. Line a 1-quart dish with
plastic wrap (if you have one, use a bowl with a
completely round base). Grease a 10-inch square and a
6-inch square cake pan and line both with waxed paper.
2 To make the cake, follow the method for preparing
enriched sponge cake in the Chef's techniques on page
63, then pour the mixture into the two cake pans and
bake for 10 minutes, or until firm to the touch. Cool on
a wire rack and peel off the waxed paper.

3 Using a flan ring, plate or cake pan as a guide, cut a
10-inch circle from the larger cake. Cut out a small
wedge (like cutting a slice of cake) to make it more
pliable and easier to fit into the round bowl. Push the
cake gently into the bowl to line it, cutting off any that
overlaps. From the second cake, cut a circle the same
size as the bowl top. Brush all the cake with the
combined liqueur and brandy.
4 To prepare the filling, beat the cream and
confectioners' sugar to soft peaks and divide between
two bowls. To the first bowl, add the nuts, chopped
chocolate and cherries. Spoon into the cake-lined bowl
and hollow out the center with the back of a spoon,
making sure the layer of cream is even. Refrigerate for
30 minutes to set.
5 Mix a third of the melted chocolate into the second
bowl of whipped cream—mixing with a little of the
cream first, before adding to the rest. Spoon into the
hollowed center of the chilled Zuccotto, level using a
metal spatula and press the circle of cake on top.
Refrigerate for 30 minutes.
6 Invert the bowl onto a wire rack and turn out the
Zuccotto. Take the remaining melted dark chocolate and
stir to cool slightly. Pour over the Zuccotto and tap the
rack to make sure the chocolate covers the whole of the
cake. Refrigerate until set. Melt the white chocolate and
flick it over the Zuccotto with a fork. Chill to allow the
Zuccotto to set before serving.

Chef's tips To roast the hazelnuts and almonds, place on
a baking sheet and bake in the oven at 350°F for about
3–5 minutes, taking care not to let the nuts burn.

To melt the chocolate, place it in the top of a double
boiler over a pan of hot water, removed from the heat.
The steaming water will gently warm and then melt the
chocolate.

Tiramisù

Layers of ladyfingers soaked in coffee and Kahlua, rich mascarpone cream and a generous dusting of cocoa powder have contributed to the enormous success of this dessert today.

Preparation time **35 minutes + chilling**
Total cooking time **None**
Serves 4–6

3 egg yolks
1/2 cup sugar
3/4 cup mascarpone cheese
1 1/4 cups whipping cream
1/4 cup Kahlúa
2 cups strong coffee, cooled
36 ladyfingers
cocoa powder, for dusting

1 Beat the egg yolks with the sugar until the sugar has dissolved and the mixture is light. Add the mascarpone and mix well. Beat the cream into stiff peaks and gently fold into the mascarpone mixture, then spread a thin layer of the mascarpone cream over the base of a deep 14-inch oval dish.

2 Add the Kahlúa to the coffee. Dip the ladyfingers into the coffee, soaking them well. Depending on the freshness of the ladyfingers, they may require more or less soaking, but be careful not too oversoak. Arrange a layer of ladyfingers close together in the dish—you may need to break them to fit the shape of your dish. Cover with another layer of the mascarpone cream, then another layer of ladyfingers, arranging them in the opposite direction to the first layer. Repeat the layers, finishing with mascarpone cream. Smooth the top and keep chilled until ready to serve. Generously dust with cocoa powder just before serving. Tiramisù is best made several hours in advance so that the flavors have time to blend before serving.

Baked peaches with mascarpone cream

*As each sealed parcel is opened, the tantalizing aroma is a
preview of the delicious flavor captured within.*

Preparation time **20 minutes**
Total cooking time **20 minutes**
Serves 4

1 1/2 tablespoons unsalted butter
1 1/2 tablespoons sugar
1 egg, lightly beaten
4 teaspoons all-purpose flour
2 tablespoons ground almonds
   (almond meal)
1 drop almond extract
2 fresh peaches, peeled and halved,
   or 4 canned peach halves
2 tablespoons sliced almonds, toasted
   (see Chef's tip)
2 tablespoons Cointreau, Kirsch
   or Grand Marnier
ground cinnamon, to dust

MASCARPONE CREAM
2/3 cup mascarpone
1/2 cup heavy cream
2 teaspoons sugar
4 drops vanilla extract
4 drops Cointreau

1 Cut out four circles of foil, 2 1/2 inches bigger all around than the peach halves. Preheat the oven to 350°F. To make the almond filling, beat together the butter and sugar until smooth. Beat in half the egg until well incorporated and mix in the flour—the mixture should be smooth and pale. Stir in the ground almonds and almond extract and beat in enough of the remaining egg to give a soft mixture that just holds its shape.

2 Place each peach half, cut-side-up, in the center of a circle of foil. Put the almond filling into a pastry bag fitted with a plain nozzle and pipe a good mound into each peach half, or spoon the mixture in neatly, filling the space where the stone was. Sprinkle with the sliced almonds, drizzle with the liqueur and dust with a pinch of cinnamon.

3 Fold up the foil around the peach halves and twist along the edges to seal. Place on a baking sheet, sealed-side-up, and bake for 15 minutes, or until the parcels have puffed. Remove the peaches from the parcels, or just open the sealed top, to serve.

4 To make the mascarpone cream, beat together all the ingredients until smooth and thick. Serve with the peach parcels.

Chef's tip To toast the almonds, place on a baking sheet and bake in a 350°F oven for 1–2 minutes.

Chocolate hazelnut torte

The toasted hazelnut meringue is enhanced by a chocolate, hazelnut mousse that is lightly set and used to fill and coat the torte.

Preparation time **40 minutes + chilling**
Total cooking time **20 minutes**
Serves 8

HAZELNUT MERINGUE

2 egg whites
1/4 cup sugar
1/2 cup lightly toasted hazelnuts, ground
  (see Chef's tip)

HAZELNUT MOUSSE

1/4 cup sugar
3 eggs
1 teaspoon gelatin powder
1 tablespoon cocoa powder
5 oz. good-quality semisweet chocolate, melted
2 oz. chocolate hazelnut spread
1/4 cup unsalted butter, beaten until soft
3/4 cup whipping cream

1/2 cup roasted hazelnuts, chopped
  (see Chef's tip)
cocoa powder and confectioners' sugar, to dust

1 Preheat the oven to 325°F. To make the hazelnut meringue, draw three 8-inch circles on waxed paper and place on a baking sheet. Beat the egg whites to firm peaks, sprinkle with the sugar and beat until stiff. Fold in the hazelnuts. Divide the mixture among the three circles and spread with the back of a spoon. Bake for 7 minutes, or until golden brown and dry. Cool on a wire rack.

2 Put the sugar with 2 tablespoons water in a small saucepan and bring slowly to a boil. Boil for 6 minutes, or until the sugar syrup reaches 240°F on a sugar thermometer, or a little forms a soft ball when dropped into cold water. Put the eggs in a large bowl and begin to beat. Pour in the bubbling syrup, aiming between the beaters and the side of the bowl. Beat constantly until a firm trail is left when the beaters are lifted.

3 Soften the gelatin in a little water, then stir over hot water until dissolved. Pour the gelatin onto the warm egg mixture, add the cocoa, chocolate and chocolate hazelnut spread and beat well. Add the butter and mix until smooth. Lightly beat the cream, then fold into the mixture and chill until thickened.

4 Spread a thick layer of mousse over two of the meringue disks, layer one upon the other and put the remaining meringue on top. Cover the top and the side with the remaining mousse, making peaks with a knife. Chill. Press the hazelnuts around the side and sprinkle a few on the top. Dust with the cocoa, then with the confectioners' sugar.

Chef's tip To toast the hazelnuts, place on a baking sheet and bake in an oven at 350°F for 3–5 minutes, taking care not to let the nuts burn.

Zabaglione with ladyfingers

This deliciously light Zabaglione must be eaten immediately after it is made.
It takes only a few minutes to make and serve and is perfect for unexpected guests.

Preparation time **15 minutes**
Total cooking time **20 minutes**
Serves 4–5

LADYFINGERS
2 eggs, separated
1/4 cup sugar
1/2 cup all-purpose flour
confectioners' sugar, to dust

ZABAGLIONE
4 egg yolks
1/3 cup sugar
1/4 cup Marsala

1 Preheat the oven to 400°F. Line a baking sheet with waxed paper. Fit a pastry bag with a 1/2-inch plain nozzle.

2 To make the ladyfingers, beat the egg yolks and sugar in a bowl until creamy and almost white. In a separate bowl, beat the egg whites until stiff peaks form as the beaters are lifted away. With a large metal spoon or plastic spatula, fold a third of the egg white into the yolk mixture. Sift half the flour into the yolk mixture and carefully fold in, then add another portion of egg white. Repeat with the remaining flour and egg white, taking care not to overmix. Spoon the mixture into the pastry bag and pipe 3-inch lengths slightly apart on the baking sheet. Dust liberally with the sifted confectioners' sugar, then leave at room temperature for 5 minutes to dissolve the sugar and create a pearl effect. Bake for 10 minutes, or until golden brown. Remove the fingers from the tray by lifting the waxed paper with the ladyfingers, then placing them upside-down on the work surface. Sprinkle the back of the paper with water to make it easy to peel away. Turn the fingers over and cool on a wire rack.

3 To make the Zabaglione, bring a saucepan half-full of water to a boil, then turn the heat as low as possible. Beat the egg yolks and sugar in a heatproof bowl until almost white. Mix in the Marsala. Place the bowl over the barely steaming water and beat until the mixture increases to four times its volume and is firm and frothy. Pour into four large wine glasses and serve immediately with the ladyfingers.

Chef's tip Zabaglione is an excellent standby dessert for unexpected guests. If you do not have the traditional Italian Marsala, use Madeira instead.

Chef's techniques

◆

Making pasta

See the list of ingredients in each pasta recipe to find out the quantity of flour, salt, olive oil and eggs needed to make the pasta dough for each dish. Fresh pasta should be used on the same day it is made.

Place the flour, salt, olive oil and eggs in a food processor and mix in short bursts until the mixture forms large crumbs.

Fold the sheet into thirds and pass through the machine again at the thickest setting. Repeat this rolling and folding ten times, lightly flouring the pasta dough and machine to prevent sticking.

Gently press the mixture between your finger and thumb to check if it will come together smoothly. If not, continue to process for a few bursts.

Without folding, continue to pass the dough through progressively thinner settings, until it has passed through the finest setting. Repeat with the remaining portions of dough.

Turn out onto a lightly floured surface and knead for 2 minutes into a smooth dough. Wrap in plastic wrap and refrigerate for 20 minutes. Secure a pasta machine to the edge of a table.

To make tagliatelle, adjust the roller settings to cut to the width stated in the recipe. Pass each sheet of dough through the lightly floured cutters. Lay in a single layer on a floured towel hanging over the back of a chair.

Divide the dough into two or four pieces. Keep covered and work with one piece at a time. Flatten into a rectangle and roll through the lightly floured pasta machine on the thickest setting.

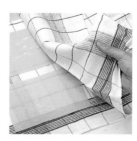
To make lasagne noodles, cut the pasta sheets to the size stated in the recipe and place side-by-side on a towel. Cover with another towel and leave until ready to use.

Preparing whole artichokes

You can cook either the whole artichoke, as shown below, or just the heart. Both are delicious.

Break off the artichoke stalk at the bottom, pulling out the fibers that attach it to the base.

Pull off the outer leaves and place the artichoke in a pan of boiling salted water with the juice of 1 lemon. Weigh down with a plate and simmer for 20–35 minutes.

Test for doneness by pulling at one of the leaves. If it comes away easily, the artichoke is done. Cut off the top half of the artichoke and discard.

Remove the hairy choke in the middle of the artichoke with a spoon. The artichoke bottom is now ready to use.

Enriched sponge cake

A sponge enriched with melted butter has a moist texture and can be plain or flavored with cocoa.

Beat the eggs and sugar in a large bowl over a pan of steaming water until the mixture is light and frothy and leaves a trail. Remove the bowl from the pan and beat until the mixture is cold.

Fold the sifted dry ingredients (flour and, if using, cocoa powder) into the mixture with a large metal spoon, being careful not to overfold and lose volume.

Pour the cooled, melted butter down the side of the bowl and gently fold in, being careful not to lose any volume.

First published in the United States in 1998 by Periplus Editions (HK) Ltd., with editorial offices at
153 Milk Street, Boston, Massachusetts 02109.

Murdoch Books and Le Cordon Bleu thank the 32 masterchefs of all the Le Cordon Bleu Schools, whose knowledge and expertise have made this book possible, especially: Chef Cliche (MOF), Chef Terrien, Chef Boucheret, Chef Duchêne (MOF), Chef Guillut, Chef Steneck, Paris; Chef Males, Chef Walsh, Chef Hardy, London; Chef Chantefort, Chef Bertin, Chef Jambert, Chef Honda, Tokyo; Chef Salembien, Chef Boutin, Chef Harris, Sydney; Chef Lawes, Adelaide; Chef Guiet, Chef Denis, Ottawa. Of the many students who helped the Chefs test each recipe, a special mention to graduates David Welch and Allen Wertheim. A very special acknowledgment to Directors Susan Eckstein, Great Britain, and Kathy Shaw, Paris, who have been responsible for the coordination of the Le Cordon Bleu team throughout this series.

The Publisher and Le Cordon Bleu also wish to thank Carole Sweetnam for her help with this series.

First published in Australia in 1998 by Murdoch Books®

Managing Editor: Kay Halsey
Series Concept, Design and Art Direction: Juliet Cohen
Editor: Jane Price
Food Director: Jody Vassallo
Food Editors: Roslyn Anderson, Tracy Rutherford
US Editor: Linda Venturoni Wilson
Designer: Michèle Lichtenberger
Photographer: Joe Filshie
Food Stylist: Carolyn Fienberg
Food Preparation: Jo Forrest
Chef's Techniques Photographers: Reg Morrison, Tim Cole
Home Economists: Michelle Lawton, Kerrie Mullins, Justine Poole, Kerrie Ray

©Design and photography Murdoch Books® 1998
©Text Le Cordon Bleu 1998. The moral right of Le Cordon Bleu has been asserted with respect to this publication.

All rights reserved. No part of this publication may be reproduced or utilized in any form or by any means, electronic or mechanical, including photocopying, recording, or by any information storage and retrieval system, without prior written permission from Periplus Editions

Library of Congress catalog card number: 98-85714
ISBN 962-593-441-3

Front cover: Tomato and balsamic vinegar salad

Distributed in the United States by
Charles E. Tuttle Co., Inc.
RR1 Box 231-5
North Clarendon, VT 05759
Tel: (802) 773-8930
Fax: (802) 773-6993

Printed in Singapore

05 04 03 02 01 00 99 98 10 9 8 7 6 5 4 3 2 1

Important: Some of the recipes in this book may include raw eggs, which can cause salmonella poisoning. Those who might be at risk from this (the elderly, pregnant women, young children and those suffering from immune deficiency diseases) should check with their physicians before eating raw eggs.